T

Rudest

‹place names

**by Stewart Ferris
and Alastair Williams**

Crombie Jardine
PUBLISHING LIMITED

13 Nonsuch Walk, Cheam, Surrey, SM2 7LG

www.crombiejardine.com

This edition was first published by
Crombie Jardine Publishing Limited in 2005

ISBN 1-905102-49-6

Written and designed by
Stewart Ferris and Alastair Williams

Printed and bound in the United Kingdom by
William Clowes Ltd, Beccles, Suffolk

Important note:
The country locations shown on the maps in this book
are approximate and their accuracy should not be relied
upon by airline pilots, explorers or invading armies.

Contents

Albania	4	Moldova	57
Algeria	6	Myanmar	58
Australia	7	Netherlands	59
Austria	14	New Zealand	60
Azerbaijan	15	Nicaragua	61
Belgium	16	Nigeria	64
Brazil	19	Norway	65
Bulgaria	20	Northern Ireland	66
Canada	21	Pakistan	67
China	26	Papua New Guinea	68
Ethiopia	28	Philippines	69
France	29	Reunion Island	72
Germany	33	Romania	73
Haiti	37	Russia	75
Hong Kong	38	Sierra Leone	78
Iceland	39	Spain	79
India	40	Sudan	82
Indian Ocean	45	Sweden	83
Indonesia	46	Switzerland	84
Iran	48	Thailand	86
Ireland	50	Turkey	88
Italy	52	Uganda	90
Japan	53	United States	91
Liberia	55	West Indies	119
Lithuania	56	Zimbabwe	120

CRAP

Albania

4

FIST

Albania

5

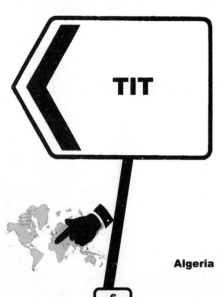

TIT

Algeria

6

BUMBANG

Australia

The world's **Rudest** place names

COCKBURN

Australia

8

CHINAMAN'S KNOB

Australia

9

IRON KNOB

Australia

10

MOUNT MEE

Australia

11

TITTYBONG

Australia

12

WET BEAVER CREEK

Australia

FUCKING

Austria

BUM

Azerbaijan

LABIA

Belgium

16

MINGE

Belgium

17

SPURT

Belgium

18

CUM

Brazil

19

SEMEN

Bulgaria

CROTCH LAKE

Canada

DILDO

Canada

SHITAGOO LAKE

Canada

PECKER'S POINT

Canada

VIRGIN ARM

Canada

25

FUKU

China

26

WANGQUING

China

Ethiopia

CLAM

France

CONDOM

France

PIS

France

31

PUSSY

France

32

TITTING

Germany

33

TITZ

Germany

34

TÖS

Germany

35

WANK

Germany

MINGE

Haiti

TONG FUK

Hong Kong

HORN

Iceland

39

CUMBUM

India

DIKSHIT

India

DONG

India

POO

India

43

WANKENER

India

The world's **Rudest** place names

SHAG ISLAND

Indian Ocean

45

ANUS

Indonesia

46

SEMEN

Indonesia

GASH

Iran

SHIT

Iran

COCKTOWN

Ireland

50

NOBBER

Ireland

ARSOLI

Italy

FUKUE >

Japan

FUKEM

Japan

54

PEE

Liberia

MINGE

Lithuania

SEMEN

Moldova

57

MOIST

Myanmar

58

BOTTOM

Netherlands

The world's **Rudest** place names

SHAG
POINT

New Zealand

CUM

Nicaragua

The world's Rudest place names

PIS PIS RIVER

Nicaragua

62

WANKS RIVER

Nicaragua

63

GISUM

Nigeria

64

BASTARD >

Norway

MUFF

Northern Ireland

66

KUNT

Pakistan

URIN

**Papua
New Guinea**

ANUS

Philippines

69

BOLLOCK

Philippines

SEXMOAN

Philippines

71

LE TAMPON

Reunion Island

CLIT

Romania

TURDO

Romania

74

TIT

Russia

TOS

Russia

VAGINA

Russia

BUM

Sierra Leone

CUNT >

Spain

79

The world's **Rudest** place names

PIS

Spain

The world's **Rudest** place names

POO

Spain

81

SHAGG

Sudan

SLUT >

Sweden

83

CUNTER

Switzerland

TITLESS

Switzerland

DONG

Thailand

The world's **Rudest** place names

PHUKET

Thailand

CUNT

Turkey

SEYMEN

Turkey

POKE

Uganda

90

BALD KNOB

United States

BALLVILLE

United States

BEAVER

United States

The world's **Rudest** place names

BIG
BEAVER

United States

94

BUMPASS

United States

CLAM

United States

CLIMAX

United States

97

COCKLAND

United States

CUMMING

United States

DICK

United States

DYCKES-VILLE

United States

ERECT

United States

FANNY

United States

FELCH

United States

FELCH-VILLE

United States

105

FRENCH LICK

United States

GLASS-COCK

United States

107

HOOKER

United States

INTER-COURSE

United States

MIANUS

United States

The world's Rudest place names

MOORHEAD

United States

MUFF

United States

PROBE

United States

113

REDDICK

United States

114

SHAFTER

United States

SUGAR TIT

United States

ONACOCK

United States

WANKERS CORNER

United States

LITTLE DIX VILLAGE

West Indies

The world's **Rudest** place names

WANKIE

Zimbabwe

**Other humour titles
from Crombie Jardine...**

Britain's Rudest place names

Stewart Ferris
& Alastair Williams

ISBN 1-905102-48-8, £2.99

Shag
your way to
the top

the real fast track to success

Imah Goer

ISBN 1-905102-17-8, £2.99

Shag

yourself slim

The most enjoyable way to lose weight

Imah Goer

ISBN 1-905102-03-8, £2.99

ISBN 1-905102-21-6, £2.99

The Little Book of
Chav speak

LEE BOK

ISBN 1-905102-20-8, £2.99

The Little Book of Chavs

The Branded Guide to Britain's New Elite

LEE BOK

ISBN 1-905102-01-1, £2.99